797,885 Books
are available to read at

www.ForgottenBooks.com

Forgotten Books' App
Available for mobile, tablet & eReader

ISBN 978-0-243-15552-1
PIBN 10663437

This book is a reproduction of an important historical work. Forgotten Books uses state-of-the-art technology to digitally reconstruct the work, preserving the original format whilst repairing imperfections present in the aged copy. In rare cases, an imperfection in the original, such as a blemish or missing page, may be replicated in our edition. We do, however, repair the vast majority of imperfections successfully; any imperfections that remain are intentionally left to preserve the state of such historical works.

Forgotten Books is a registered trademark of FB &c Ltd.
Copyright © 2017 FB &c Ltd.
FB &c Ltd, Dalton House, 60 Windsor Avenue, London, SW19 2RR.
Company number 08720141. Registered in England and Wales.

For support please visit www.forgottenbooks.com

1 MONTH OF FREE READING

at

www.ForgottenBooks.com

By purchasing this book you are eligible for one month membership to ForgottenBooks.com, giving you unlimited access to our entire collection of over 700,000 titles via our web site and mobile apps.

To claim your free month visit:
www.forgottenbooks.com/free663437

* Offer is valid for 45 days from date of purchase. Terms and conditions apply.

English
Français
Deutsche
Italiano
Español
Português

www.forgottenbooks.com

Mythology Photography **Fiction**
Fishing Christianity **Art** Cooking
Essays Buddhism Freemasonry
Medicine **Biology** Music **Ancient Egypt** Evolution Carpentry Physics
Dance Geology **Mathematics** Fitness
Shakespeare **Folklore** Yoga Marketing
Confidence Immortality Biographies
Poetry **Psychology** Witchcraft
Electronics Chemistry History **Law**
Accounting **Philosophy** Anthropology
Alchemy Drama Quantum Mechanics
Atheism Sexual Health **Ancient History**
Entrepreneurship Languages Sport
Paleontology Needlework Islam
Metaphysics Investment Archaeology
Parenting Statistics Criminology
Motivational

1928-1929

HONORARY MEMBERS

Mrs. Henry Cockshutt
Miss M. S. Cooke (Japan)
Mrs. William I. Ross

LIFE MEMBERS

Mrs. A. E. Ames
Miss M. S. Cooke
Mrs. A. L. Davis
Mrs. Timothy Eaton
Mrs. Frank Morley
Mrs. Helen G. MacMath
Mr. Percival Ricout

BOARD OF MANAGEMENT

Miss Mortimer Clark
Mrs. Ambrose Kent
Mrs. J. P. Balfour
Mrs. A. M. Cowan
Mrs. Wm. Davidson
Lady Hearst
Mrs. Stewart Houston
Mrs. Wm. Inglis
Mrs. H. H. Love

Miss Grant Macdonald
Miss Effie Michie
Miss J. M. McGee
Mrs. Wm. Sparks
Mr. John Firstbrook
Mr. W. A. Baird, K.C., M.P.P.
Mr. S. B. Gundy
Dr. Edmund E. King
Dr. W. H. Harris

Rev. Canon Bryan
Mr. G. O. Fleming
Ven. Archdeacon Ingles
Mr. W. G. Kent
Mr. E. J. Lennox
Mr. Allen Neilson
Rev. Basil Thompson
Mr. George Wilson
His Worship, The Mayor

MEDICAL STAFF

Consulting Physicians

H. B. Anderson, M.D.
W. T. Burns, M.D.
Geo. Carveth, M.D.

J. E. Elliott, M.D.
E. E. King, M.D.
N. A. Powell, M.D.

W. B. Thistle, M.D.
F. N. Winnett, M.D.
W. A. Young, M.D.

Visiting Physicians

A. C. Bennett, M.D.
F. A. Clarkson, M.D.
C. J. Copp, M.D.

Jos. S. Graham, M.D.
R. C. Griffith, M.D.
J. H. Hart, M.D.

A. A. Jackson, M.D.
Julian Loudon, M.D.
Brefney O'Reilly, M.D.

Relief Staff

C. H. Archibald, M.D.
Harold Ball, M.D.
Eleanor Bennett, M.D.
E. C. Beer, M.D.
E. C. Burson, M.D.
W. F. Clarke, M.D.
John Duncan, M.D.
J. H. Elliott, M.D.
W. E. Ferguson, M.D.

G. J. Gillam, M.D.
C. H. Gilmour, M.D.
Charles Harris, M.D.
F. R. Hassard, M.D.
G. D. Jeffs, M.D.
J. E. Knox, M.D.
J. H. Lawson, M.D.
Julian Loudon, M.D.

F. C. Marlow, Jr., M.D.
W. L. C. MacBeth, M.D.
A. F. Mavety, M.D.
W. J. O'Hara, M.D.
W. H. Robertson, M.D.
F. W. Rolph, M.D.
Chas. Sheard, Jr., M.D.
H. M. Tovell, M.D.
C. S. Wright, M.D.

Specialists

Edmund E. King, M.D., L.R.C.P. Lond., Chairman Medical Board
W. H. Harris, M.D., Secretary Medical Board
G. H. Burnham, M.D. Oculist and Aurist
W. H. Lowry, M.D., Oculist and Aurist
Mortimer Lyon, M.D., Oculist and Aurist
W. L. Robinson, M.D., Assoc. Prof. Pathology, Toronto University
F. C. Trebilcock, M.D., Oculist and Aurist
C. A. Wells, M.D., Pathologist
N. K. Wilson, M.D., Oto-Laryngolosist.

OFFICERS

President—Mr. John Firstbrook,
Vice-President— Mr. W. A. Baird, K.C., M.P.P.
Vice-President— Mr. S. B. Gundy,
Lady Directress— Miss Mortimer Clark,
Lady Directress— Mrs. Ambrose Kent.

TRUSTEES

Mr. John Firstbrook
Mr. W. A. Baird
Mr. S. B. Gundy

EXECUTIVE COMMITTEE

Miss Mortimer Clark
Mrs. Ambrose Kent
Mrs. J. P. Balfour
Mrs. A. M. Cowan
Mrs. Wm. Davidson

Lady Hearst
Mrs. Wm. Inglis
Miss Effie Michie
Miss Grant Macdonald
Mr. John Firstbrook

Mr. W. A. Baird, K.C., M.P.P.
Mr. S. B. Gundy
Mr. G. O. Fleming
Ven. Archdeacon Ingles
Mr. E. J. Lennox
Mr. George Wilson

HOUSE STAFF

Miss Esther M. Cook, Lady Superintendent
Miss Ida Zella Groat, Secretary-Treasurer
Miss Margaret M. Bowman, Housekeeper
Miss Annie M. Coulter, Dietitian
Dr. Frederick C. Harrison, House Physician.

MR. JOHN FIRSTBROOK

ELECTED MEMBER OF THE BOARD OF MANAGEMENT IN 1917,
VICE-PRESIDENT IN 1925,
PRESIDENT IN 1926

FIFTY-FOURTH ANNUAL MEETING
OF THE
TORONTO HOSPITAL
FOR INCURABLES

The Fifty-Fourth Annual Meeting of the Toronto Hospital for Incurables was held at the Hospital on Friday afternoon, October 26th, 1928, at three o'clock.

The Meeting was opened with Devotional Exercises conducted by the Rev. Dr. Bryan.

The President, Mr. John Firstbrook, occupied the chair and with him on the platform was the Hon. Mr. Ross, Lieutenant Governor of Ontario.

Reports were presented by Miss Cook, Superintendent; Dr. Edmund E. King, Chairman of the Medical Board, and Miss Groat, Secretary-Treasurer.

A Resolution was moved by Mr. Firstbrook, seconded by Mr. Baird,—That the Reports as presented be adopted and printed for distribution, which was carried unanimously.

A Resolution was moved by Dr. King, seconded by Mr. Fred Ratcliff, and carried unanimously, naming the Board of Management for the ensuing year.

A short address was given by His Honour, Mr. Ross, after which Miss Cook presented Mrs. Ross with a handsome bouquet of chrysanthemums.

The National Anthem was sung, following which a Reception was held by Miss Mortimer Clark, Mrs. Ambrose Kent, and Miss Cook in the Lady Mortimer Clark Residence for Nurses, where refreshments were served.

OPENING ADDRESS

THE CHAIRMAN (Mr. John Firstbrook): I am sure you will all agree with me, ladies and gentlemen, that we are highly favoured in having with us this afternoon His Honour the Lieutenant Governor and Mrs. Ross. It is very gracious of them to give of their time to be here, and I am sure that their presence will be a great encouragement to us in attending to the labours that we have in hand. (Applause.)

I now call on Rev. Dr. Bryan to open our meeting.
(Devotional exercises.)

REPORT OF THE MEDICAL BOARD

October, 1928

In presenting the Annual Medical Report I have much pleasure in announcing that we have during the year increased our bed capacity by seventy-five beds, making at present a total of 325 beds available. We have accomplished this by taking over and remodelling the West wing, which was formerly the Nurses' Residence, and also by taking over the space occupied by the employees and transferring them to better and more desirable quarters over the new Power Plant. This has been our desire, and a necessity, for a long period of time and has only just now come to fruition.

The Cameron wing, also known as the Cancer wing, has been renovated, brightened and the ventilation improved and has a capacity of 18 beds. At the present time we have a Cancer population of 10.

The general admission to the Hospital for the past year has been 116, their numerous diseases are tabulated and attached to this report.

There occurred in the Hospital 72 deaths, which is rather a low death rate, particularly when we see 16 of these occurred from Hemiplegia (Apoplexy) and 16 from Cancer. The summary in this particular respect is that at September 30th, 1927, there was a population of 223 and at the end of this year there was a population of 253, which is an increase of 30. We had 14 patients discharged for reasons—improvement, desire to leave, etc.

It has been a desire of the Government to supervise the patients of all Public Institutions and check up on the necessity for their remaining in the Institution as charges on the Government. It has required filling up a very large form, and a great number of questions (24), and a summary of the needs and requirements of each.

This has necessitated a great deal of labor, and at the present time it is almost completed. This, of course, will not have to be repeated because it is the intention to have this form filled in when the patient is admitted, leaving only the summary of attention to be filled in at the end of each year.

It has been very difficult at times deciding on the admission of certain applicants; those who had incurable maladies yet not requiring active medical care; those who had attained old age from 70-90 with such things as paralysis; those able to go about and attend to their wants at the homes of friends or relatives; and it has been very hard to refuse certain cases, but it is necessary at times, so that the beds will not be crowded by those who are not seriously ill.

The word Incurable does not apply in reality to this Institution, as by treatment and massage ten have been so much improved that they have been able to leave the Institution; not better but much improved.

There are at present in the Hospital a few waiting the decision of the Government as to their disposal. The lack of facilities for Aged Persons Homes is very marked in the Province. We will undoubtedly have to carry these people until the Government can secure proper accommodation for them.

The Medical supervision of all the inmates of the Hospital is under the supervision of Dr. F. C. Harrison, who devotes a considerable time each day to this duty, and the members of the staff also attend to a visiting period each month.

The Medical Board recommend the appointment of Dr. C. A. Wells as an addition to the Staff, and also the appointment of Dr. W. L. Robinson as pathologist.

The investigation of Cancer, its cause and treatment is at the present time very active in the medical world, and it is to be hoped that the Hospital for Incurables will be able to supply some data from which these ends may be helped in their attainment.

During the past year the Staff has lost one of its active members, Dr. Allen Adams, who is removed in the prime of health by the dread scourge, pneumonia.

With our present buildings and dwelling accommodation for the nursing staff we are probably as well equipped to-day as any Institution of its kind in the Dominion.

The patients are all cheerful and appreciate the kindly attention of all the members of the Staff. Complaints must arise, but they are exceedingly few and in most cases easily met.

The members of the permanent staff, the Superintendent, Miss Cook, the Housekeeper, Miss Bowman; the Dietition, Miss Coulter; the Head Nurse, Miss Delany, and the Secretary-Treasurer, Miss Groat, invariably aid the Staff of visiting Doctors with every courtesy and attention.

EDMUND E. KING, M.D. Tor., L.R.C.P., Lond.
Chairman Medical Board.

Admissions October 1, 1927, to September 30, 1928—116 in all—

Hemiplegia	22	Lateral Sclerosis	1
Arthritis	22	Myelitis	1
Cancer	18	Chronic Gastritis	1
Paralysis Agitans	10	Progressive Muscular Atrophy	1
Cardiovascular Diseases	10	Bulbar Paralysis	1
Fractured Hip	5	Spinal Caries	1
Disseminate Sclerosis	4	Meyxoedema	1
Locomotor Ataxia	3	Aneurysm	1
Diabetes	3	Brain Tumour	1
Poliomyelitis	2	Anaemia	1
Traumatic Myelitis	2	Osteoma	1
Paraplegia	2	Nephritis	1
Pernicious Anaemia	1		
			116

Deaths, October 1, 1927, to September 30, 1928—72 in all—

Hemiplegia	16	Paraplegia	3
Cancer	16	Tumour of Spinal Cord	1
Cardiovascular Disease	8	Toxic Adenoma	1
Paralysis Agetans	7	Disseminate Sclerosis	1
Arthritis	7	Chronic Cystitis	1
Locomotor Ataxia	5	Bulbar Paralysis	1
Fractured Hip	4	Lateral Sclerosis	1
			72

REPORT OF SUPERINTENDENT

Your Honour, Mr. President, Ladies and Gentlemen:

The year that has just come to a close has been crowded with business activities as was the previous year. The Power Plant to the north of this building, with the Laundry and accommodation for the male and female employees, was finished and occupied before Christmas. The New Annex, linking up the extra accommodation for patients made possible by reconstruction of the building vacated by the nurses, has been completed during the year and two floors are now occupied by patients. The laying of linoleum on the floors of the wards and corridors on the third floor of the Annex was left over for a time because of having ample accommodation at present without using that section and also because of the heavy expense connected with so much reconstruction.

In the Basement, the new Dining-room for employees was finished and a Demonstration Class Room for nurses arranged. The rooms formerly occupied by the

Laundry have been converted into fine storerooms and some of the old storerooms are now used by the Occupational Therapy Department for supplies.

The next step is the extension of our Kitchen which is much too small to meet the extra demands. The old gas range in the kitchen was worn out and the new one just installed this month is half as large again as the old one and should be sufficient for the extra cooking that will be needed for the additional patients.

In caring for a building of this size, especially as old a building, it is astonishing how much attention is required to keep it in a semblance of order. On the outside, each year the roof has to be gone over, the eave pipes repaired, loose bricks replaced, chimneys need attention, and this year our grounds were so badly torn up through building in so many places that considerable money had to be expended on them. For years our neighbors to the south have complained that in the Spring especially, the water from our grounds flooded their cellars and caused other damage. Before fixing the grounds a complete system of tile drainage was placed under the lawn which should help to a great extent in making the Hospital less damp and we hope it will also do away with the flooding of our neighbors' cellars. This alone was a great expense, and after the men got through we had little left of the lawn but our trees. This work and the work of turning the sod and seeding the lawn covered most of the summer months and while the patients missed having as much space as usual, as they were confined to the Dunn Avenue side, it should be very beautiful next year.

Inside, we have been more or less upset due to reconstruction and extension. As one section or department was finished it was painted and made ready for occupancy, but while the rest of the Hospital came in for routine care, that is walls and ceilings washed every few months, etc., it has been neglected in such matters as painting and other improvements. Each year there seems to be so many demands for plastering, carpentry and painting. This year many of the wards, bathrooms, pantries have needed extensive repairs in plastering and the bathrooms and serving pantries in the Main Building are being painted following the plastering. In the year to come, it will be necessary to paint many of our wards and corridors. The wards in the New Annex are very attractive and pleasant and, in order that the patients remaining in the Main Building may not feel that they have been overlooked, it will be necessary to make some changes and do considerable decorating.

Each year there is considerable outlay for beds and other articles of furniture. This year we have had to furnish the Annex as well as replace broken pieces. Many of our patients spend twenty-four hours of the day on their beds, accounting for the many beds and mattresses required to keep them comfortable.

Last year, through the generosity of the Occupational Therapy Society, we had a part time Instructress in that Department. This year we were fortunate in securing the full time service of Miss Lindsay, who has established that Department here and is gradually interesting a few more patients. They now occupy the room in the basement at the south below the verandahs but we hope before long to be able to enclose with glass the space in readiness on the roof of the Annex. There they will have sunshine and a beautiful view of the City and the lake.

We also hope for a Gymnasium where any who wish may take exercises and help bring back loss of power in limbs and become less helpless. The public is apt to think that we care only for the aged. We have many patients ranging from seventeen to forty-five and unless there is something to interest and help these younger members of our family, they have an empty outlook for the future. While shut-in and unable to enjoy much that the world has to offer by way of diversion and amusement, some of them put up a brave fight and get more out of life than many who are well and out in the world. Usually there is a dark period of adjustment. Then, if given half a chance and the handicap is not too great, they find something in which to take an interest and perhaps become helpful to others and, in so doing, find their happiness.

We are again indebted to the Canadian National Exhibition for free admission of patients and their escorts daily; to the Royal Winter Fair, through the kindness of Mrs. Wm. Inglis, for free entrance for forty patients to an afternoon performance in the Coliseum; to the Ontario Motor League for a delightful drive, with candy and tobacco, this September; to Mrs. R. B. Hamilton for a chicken supper followed by a concert for which the programme was arranged by Mr. Charles Ross and Mr. McCann; to the Exhibition Midway Entertainers for an afternoon's performance on our grounds; to the City Dairy Co. Limited, for ice cream for the patients and staff on several occasions; to the City Dairy Co. Band, for a concert on the lawn; to Mr. Allen Neilson for an ice cream treat; to Mrs. Wm. Inglis for furnishing patients' sitting-room, and to many others for concerts and treats, all of which have been greatly appreciated.

We appreciate greatly the willing help of the Clergy who conduct our Sunday afternoon service and minister to our patients generally. There are many very kind visitors,—I will not mention any names,—they are very unobtrusive to say the least, who come almost weekly with some little treat for some of the less fortunate members; take them for motor rides and out to church or tea, perhaps, and return them just ever so much brighter and more ready for the daily trials of an invalid. When trying to thank one of them one day, she assured me she got more happiness out of it than she could ever put in. We need just such people to take an interest in our patients. If you are not already acquainted and have an afternoon occasionally, come out and spend it with them. The Annual Sale of patients' work is on Saturday, November 24th, and they would be so happy to have you come.

We are most fortunate in having the resourceful Dr. F. C. Harrison as House Physician. He is never too busy or occupied to be interested in the slightest wish of the patients. Dr. King and the other members of the Medical Board are also always within reach if needed.

The Report of the Training School will be published in the Annual Report. While this Report deals with the Pupil Nurses, I wish to take this opportunity of expressing my appreciation, not only of the House Staff which consists of Dr. Harrison, House Physician; Miss Groat, Secretary-Treasurer; Miss Coulter, Dietitian; Miss Bowman, Housekeeper; but also the different Supervisors, the graduate and undergraduate nurses, who help make up the personnel of the Hospital. Any degree of success to which we have attained is due to their untiring efforts, their devotion to the patients and their wish to be of service to the Hospital and the Board of Management.

Faithfully submitted,

ESTHER M. COOK,
Superintendent.

REPORT OF THE SECRETARY-TREASURER

Your Honour, Mr. President, Ladies and Gentlemen:

It is my privilege to present at this Fifty-fourth Annual Meeting the Reports of the Secretary-Treasurer for the year ended September 30th, 1928.

The Board of Management, composed of twenty-seven ladies and gentlemen, meets monthly to receive applications for admission to the Hospital and to consider the financial and administration problems which have greatly increased with the enlargement of the institution. It may be information for those who are not familiar with the Hospital to give the names of the Officers, who are as follows:—President, Mr. John Firstbrook; Vice-Presidents, Mr. W. A. Baird, K.C., M.P.P., and Mr. S. B. Gundy; Lady Directresses, Miss Mortimer Clark, Mrs. Ambrose Kent, while Dr. Edmund E. King is Chairman of the Medical Board and Dr. W. H. Harris is the Secretary.

It is with sincere regret that we refer to the loss sustained by the death of Mr. Reuben Millichamp—a Member of the Board for some twenty years and a Trustee for the past ten years, who gave freely of his time and experience. We also deplore the passing of Dr. Allan Adams, who was a Member of the Medical Board for nearly twenty years and who was most generous in his service, particularly in visiting applicants for admission. The death of Lady Hendrie, an Honourary Member, was also deeply regretted as she had been most interested in the Hospital during her tenure at Government House.

At the 1st of October, 1927, there were 223 patients in the Hospital. During the year there were 116 admissions, making a total of 339 for the year; 72 deaths occurred and 14 were discharged; one woman was well enough to return to her home and two men left to resume employment, while three patients returned from the Western Hospital where they had gone for dental treatment. We greatly appreciate the hearty co-operation of the Western Hospital when we require such or any service. These statistics indicate that we have admitted 56 more patients than in the previous year and that 28 more deaths occurred. We have a number of patients who have been with us for ten to twenty years, but of those who passed away there were twenty who were here from two days to three months, while ten others were less than six months in the Hospital. It is obvious that these patients required more than ordinary nursing care. The ages of patients admitted ranged from seventeen to ninety-three years.

Our Financial Statement, audited by Clarkson, Gordon, Dilworth, Guilfoyle & Nash, with minute attention to every detail, will be published, as is customary, in the Annual Report, of which we will be pleased to send copies to all who would care to receive them. We will now give you only the outstanding features.

The total Expenditure for the year for Maintenance amounted to $226,376.21, and the Receipts included $39,518.40 from the Province of Ontario; $87,134.00 from the City of Toronto for patients on City Orders; $37,632.53 from paying patients, and $18,555.71 from subscriptions and other receipts. We commenced the year with an Overdraft of $8,360.61, and closed with an Overdraft of $3,535.57, and an indebtedness to the Bank for a loan of $40,000.

It is probable that by next Annual Meeting we will have completed payments on our new Buildings, Furnishings, Equipment, etc., that is, the contractors will have been paid but not our indebtedness to the Bank. We will then be in a position to give the complete cost of the alterations and additions. Up to the present, an expenditure of nearly $500,000 has been made on the Nurses' Residence, the Boiler House, Laundry, Dormitories and alterations in the old Nurses' Residence to get it prepared for the use of patients, the Annex connecting that Building with the Main Building and the Furnishings for all. Towards this expenditure we have received $125,000 from the Province of Ontario, the same amount from the City of Toronto, $5,905.00 in special subscriptions and $63,500 has been transferred from the Hospital Capital and Savings Account.

The need for financial assistance is greater than ever and we are hopeful that there will be a very generous response to the appeal we make annually about the end of November. We are grateful to those who have helped us in the past and feel that you are assured that the Hospital for Incurables is worthy your support. Our aim is for greater and better service.

Faithfully submitted,

IDA ZELLA GROAT,
Secretary-Treasurer.

TORONTO HOSPITAL FOR INCURABLES MAINTENANCE ACCOUNT

Statement of Cash Receipts and Disbursements for the Year Ended 30th September, 1928

RECEIPTS

FROM PROVINCE OF ONTARIO:

For quarter ended 30th September, 1927	$ 9,374.50	
For period 1st October, 1927, to 30th June, 1928	30,143.90	
		$ 39,518.40

FROM CITY OF TORONTO:

For month of September, 1927	$ 7,135.50	
For period 1st October, 1927, to 31st July, 1928	79,998.50	
		87,134.00
Patients' Board		37,632.53
Subscriptions and Collections		6,257.39
Income from Investments and Legacies	$12,135.76	
Less: Collection and other charges	78.40	
		12,057.36
Sundry Receipts		240.96
		$182,840.64

Excess of Disbursements over Receipts—

Loan from Imperial Bank of Canada	$40,000.00	
Increase in Bank Overdraft	3,535.57	
		43,535.57
		$226,376.21

Bank Account (Maintenance)

Loan from Imperial Bank		$40,000.00
Overdraft Imperial Bank, 30th September, 1927	$8,360.61	
Increase in Overdraft for year	3,535.57	
Overdraft Imperial Bank, 30th September, 1928		11,896.18
		$51,896.18
		$226,376.21

DISBURSEMENTS

Groceries and Provisions	$ 5,665.98	
Fruit—fresh and canned	8,451.92	
Vegetables	9,076.48	
Meat and Fish	15,065.23	
Eggs	5,909.92	
Butter	7,290.55	
Flour, Bread and Meal	3,959.92	
Milk	7,933.15	
Tea and Coffee	3,010.96	
Ice	1,192.96	
		$ 67,557.07
Drugs and Medicines	$ 4,752.65	
Medical Supplies	3,700.63	
		8,453.28
Furniture and Furnishings	$ 8,156.87	
Bedding and Napery	8,648.80	
Dry Goods for Patients	2,452.05	
Brooms, Brushes, Soap, etc.	6,843.07	
Nurses' Outfits	563.07	
		26,663.86
Fuel	$15,504.63	
Maintenance of Engine and Boiler	724.23	
Elevator and Laundry Power	561.38	
Light	2,360.80	
Water	1,859.47	
		21,010.51
Repairs Ordinary	$ 6,293.81	
Repairs Extraordinary	7,017.93	
Cleaning and Improving Grounds	4,815.94	
		18,127.68
Salaries and Wages	$76,938.18	
Advertising, Stationery, etc.	2,496.48	
Insurance	884.96	
Bank Charges and Interest on Loan	1,686.68	
Contingencies	2,557.51	
		84,563.81
		$226,376.21

AUDITORS' CERTIFICATE

We have audited the above statement of Cash Receipts and Disbursements on Maintenance Account for the year ended 30th September, 1928, and we certify the same to be correct.

CLARKSON, GORDON, DILWORTH, GUILFOYLE & NASH,
Chartered Accountants.

Toronto, 19th October, 1928.

Form of Bequest

I give and bequeath to the Board of Management of the Toronto Hospital for Incurables, Toronto, Ontario, the sum of $............................. (or personal property or real estate) to be used for carrying on the charitable designs of the aforesaid Institution.

AMBROSE KENT WING. CORNER STONE LAID BY SIR JAMES WHITNEY, JUNE, 1909.
OPENED BY MRS. AMBROSE KENT, OCTOBER 26th, 1910.

ADOPTION OF REPORTS

THE CHAIRMAN: Your Honour, Mrs. Ross, Ladies and Gentlemen: It is not my purpose to make any lengthy remarks, but rather to exercise my privilege of moving the adoption of the three Reports to which you have just listened. I am sure that all of you have been most intensely interested in what you have heard.

This Hospital was founded fifty-four years ago. Its first location was then much nearer the centre of the city, although relatively perhaps farther out than it is at present or has been for some years. Later, this property was purchased and the central part of the main building was erected, and it has been added to from time to time. As Miss Groat stated in her report, when all the outstanding accounts are paid we will have spent in excess of $500,000 on buildings—the nurses' residence, boiler house, laundry, quarters for our help, and the addition to connect the main building with the former nurses' residence—and even then there will still be room for further expenditures.

I should like to go into detail, but I shall not weary you with that. We see many things that can be done to improve the physical condition of the Hospital. These will take time and will require the expenditure of a great deal of money, but judging from the support we have had in the past I am sure it will be forthcoming when it is needed.

Mr. Baird, our Vice-President, will second the motion for the adoption of these three reports.

MR. BAIRD: Your Honour, Mr. President, Ladies and Gentlemen: Before formally seconding the motion for the adoption of the three most excellent Reports which have been submitted for our consideration, I should like to add my personal word of appreciation of the great compliment which has been paid this Hospital by His Honour the Lieutenant Governor and Mrs. Ross in being here this afternoon. We have indeed been honoured.

The three Reports submitted present in a concise and condensed form a record of the activities of the Hospital in its various departments during the past year. As is always the case, the Reports have been exceedingly modest and have kept in the background the splendid work which has been done personally by those who presented them.

To Dr. King, Chairman of the Medical Board, to Dr. Harris, the Secretary of that Board, and to the various well-known specialists and general practitioners throughout the city who have so kindly volunteered their services, our best thanks are due at all times. To Dr. Harrison, whose services have been mentioned in two of the reports, we are extremely grateful. Without him I scarcely know how we would be able to get along.

The report of Miss Cook, the Superintendent, is in its usual breezy, concise and helpful form. Miss Cook always has suggestions to offer for the betterment of conditions not only for the patients in the Hospital, but for the Board who endeavour to keep things running. We are always under obligation to Miss Cook for her helpful suggestions. I do not know whether she realizes it or not, but the Board depends upon her to a very great extent in all their deliberations.

To Miss Groat, too, we are extremely grateful. Her report necessarily deals with figures and statistics, which are very often somewhat dry, but I think you will agree that in her report she makes them intensely interesting. Her books are splendidly kept, her records could not be better, and although she is not always able to present a balanced budget at the end of the year I assure you it is not her fault.

I have very much pleasure in seconding the motion for the adoption of these three annual reports.

The motion was agreed to, and the reports were adopted.

ADDRESS BY THE LIEUTENANT-GOVENOR

THE CHAIRMAN: His Honour has requested a moment to speak to you. I am sure we are all delighted to accede to his request. (Applause.)

HIS HONOUR THE LIEUTENANT GOVERNOR: Mr. Chairman, Ladies and Gentlemen: This is the first request of such a nature that I have made. I am very pleased to be present at the fifty-fourth annual meeting of this institution. We are all apt to take for granted the priceless services of our clergymen, doctors, and nurses, in our hospitals. If I heard the report of the Secretary-Treasurer correctly, two of your patients left you to be married, so I am sure the doctors and nurses of this hospital are worthy of special consideration.

Your Board of Management have followed the splendid example set by their predecessors in giving personal care and thought to the affairs of this hospital. So it was in the beginning; so it is now and so may it continue until the end.

I have been very much interested in the Reports that have been presented, but my purpose in coming here was not to speak, but simply to express my appreciation, personally and officially, of what you have done, and to meet the Executive, the Members of the Board, and others interested in the great work of this institution. (Applause.)

THE CHAIRMAN: I am sure we are all deeply grateful to His Honour for his words of appreciation. They will encourage us to go on to greater heights in the work that we have undertaken.

Your Honour, on behalf of all of us, I thank you very much.

ELECTION OF BOARD OF MANAGEMENT, 1928-29

THE CHAIRMAN: The resolution nominating the Board of Management for the coming year will be moved by Dr. King:

DR. EDMUND E. KING: I move: Resolved that the following be the Board of Management for the ensuing year:

Miss Mortimer Clark
Mrs. Ambrose Kent
Mrs. J. P. Balfour
Mrs. William Davidson
Mrs. Alix. M. Cowan
Lady Hearst
Miss Grant Macdonald
Miss Effie Michie
Mrs. Stewart Houston
Mrs. William Inglis
Mrs. H. H. Love
Miss J. M. McGee
Mrs. William Sparks

Mr. John Firstbrook
Mr. W. A. Baird
Mr. S. B. Gundy
Rev. Dr. Bernard Bryan
Rev. Dr. C. L. Ingles
Mr. G. O. Fleming
Dr. W. H. Harris
Dr. Edmund E. King
Mr. W. G. Kent
Mr. E. J. Lennox
Mr. Allen Neilson
Rev. Basil Thompson
Mr. George Wilson
His Worship the Mayor

MR. FRED RATCLIFF: Mr. President, I have very much pleasure in seconding this resolution.

While His Honour was speaking, I was thinking what a pity it is that more of our citizens do not know more about the Hospital for Incurables. I suppose that practically all of them know there is such a place; but if they would only come out here once and go through the institution, I am satisfied that there would be a great deal more interest shown in the work here.

I am indeed glad to have the opportunity of seconding this resolution, because in looking over the list I see the names of many successful business men whose experience, I am sure, must be a great asset to this institution. Without detracting at all from the work done by the Superintendent and the medical faculty, I may be allowed to say that I think we all owe a debt of gratitude to the President, and that

I do not think better men could be found to conduct the very important work that is being carried on here

THE CHAIRMAN: I am grateful for your kindly reference.

Before putting the motion, I might say to Mr. Ratcliff that it is a great pleasure to us to have those connected with other hospitals interested in our hospital. Mr. Ratcliff is Treasurer of the Wellesley Hospital. I had hoped that the Chairman of the Board of Toronto General Hospital would be here this afternoon, but at the last moment we received a note saying that a very important meeting there prevented his coming.

Is it your pleasure to adopt the motion?

The motion was agreed to, and the resolution was adopted.

ADJOURNMENT

THE CHAIRMAN: We usually have special addresses on this occasion, but this year we have curtailed the meeting somewhat. We hope that when you leave here you will proceed to the Lady Mortimer Clark Residence for Nurses to partake of the refreshments which have been provided and to spend a short time in social intercourse. We also would like you to go through the Hospital so that you may have some idea of what has been done during the past few months.

A bouquet of flowers having been presented to Mrs. Ross, the National Anthem was sung, after which those present adjourned to the Lady Mortimer Clark Residence for Nurses where refreshments were served.

REPORT OF THE GRANT MACDONALD TRAINING SCHOOL FOR NURSES

MAY 18th, 1928

Mr. Chairman, Members of the Graduating Class, Ladies and Gentlemen:

In presenting a brief Report of the Training School, I wish to give you an outline of the history of the School. While the Hospital, which started as a Home on Bathurst Street in the year 1872, a'ways had a nurse and attendants for the patients, it was not until 1903 that the Training School for Nurses was organized. In 1906 the name of the institution was changed to "Hospita' for Incurables" and later an Affiliated Course was arranged with Bellevue and Allied Hospitals, New York City, so that the students now have two months Acute Medical and Surgical Nursing, two months Pediatrics, two months Obstetrics, two months Operating Room and two months Out Patients' Department or Emergency experience.

The Students in the Junior and Senior Years have the advantage of the Centralized Lecture Course at the University of Toronto, with a short course in Massage and one month's practical experience in the Public Health Department.

The Teaching and Supervising Staff is composed of Miss Hiscocks as part time Instructress; Miss Delany, who assists with the teaching as well as the Supervising; Miss Coulter, B.A., who gives a course in Dietetics, Invalid Cookery, and the Misses Lynch, Lawson and Forman, who assist with the Supervising.

We have in the Training School nine students, who are graduating to-night; seventeen students in Affiliation in New York; eighteen students in the Junior Year and ten probationers. We also have 8 Graduate Nurses in charge of the different Departments, and a few other nurses who assist with the routine ward work and care of the patients.

The constant demand for extra beds for patients made it necessary to extend the Hospital and since the Nurses' Residence was near enough to connect up and remodel for additional wards, it was considered advisable to build another residence for nurses. It has taken considerable time to do all the reconstruction and building connected with making this extension but we now have desirable accommodation for about one hundred nurses and will soon increase our bed capacity for patients from 240 to 300 beds.

I cannot speak too highly of the valuable service rendered the Hospital, not only by the students in training, but by the graduates and outside nurses on our Staff. At best the work is discouraging and the nurses who make a success of it must have unusual qualifications.

On behalf of the Staff, I wish to congratulate the Graduating Class and assure them of our sincere best wishes and of our continued interest in their future work. We trust you will not become indifferent or disinterested and think that it is all over just because you no longer attend Classes. We have tried to create in you the desire for knowledge,—tried to give you a practical interest in your associates and the sick entrusted to your care,—tried to help you develop into useful, capable women. We trust you will continue your interest in your studies. Perhaps you may take a Post Graduate Course in some special work that appeals to you most but, in any event, we trust you will continue to read books of educational value. If you come up to our expectations for you, the Training School will have reason to be proud of you.

Faithfully submitted,

ESTHER M. COOK,
Superintendent.

GRANT MACDONALD TRAINING SCHOOL FOR NURSES
Graduation Exercises, May 18th, 1928
Chairman, Mr. John Firstbrook

March .... Miss Edith Dolson
Invocation .... Rev. Mr. Amos
Superintendent's Report .... Miss Cook
Address .... Rev. Mr. F. C. Vesey
Presentation of Diplomas and School Pins .... Miss Mortimer Clark

Presentation of Mr. Ambrose Kent's Gold Medal for Highest Standing in the Final Examinations—Awarded to Miss Jean A. Macpherson. Presented by Mrs. Ambrose Kent.

Prize for Second place in the Final Examinations.—Awarded to Mrs. Caroline M. Ash. Presented by Miss Mortimer Clark, the donor.

Prize for Highest Standing in Dietetics—given by Miss Coulter, B.A.—Awarded to Miss Jean A. Macpherson. Presented by Miss Hiscocks.

Prize for Neatness and General Efficiency.—Awarded to Mrs. Caroline M. Ash. Presented by the donor—Mrs. R. B. Hamilton.

Presentation of Hypodermic Syringes to the Graduates—the gift of the Alumnae Association. Presented by Miss Taylor, President.

God Save the King.

Reception.
Dancing.

GRADUATES, 1928

Miss Ethel Mildred Johnson, Oshawa, Ontario
Miss Isabel Frances Dunn, Lower Melbourne, Quebec
Miss Jean Anastasia Macpherson, Toronto, Ontario
Miss Katherine Esther Murchison, Toronto, Ontario
Mrs. Caroline Maude Ash, Toronto, Ontario
Miss Rosalind Katherine Yohn, Cache Bay, Ontario
Miss Amy Isabel Poff, Cache Bay, Ontario
Miss Ruth Isobel Paul, Cache Bay, Ontario
Miss Lera Alecia Empey, Brockville, Ontario

LADY MORTIMER CLARK RESIDENCE FOR NURSES

ENTERTAINMENTS

Concert, given by Rev. Mr. Stanger and Y.P.A. of Church of Ascension.
Travelogue—Mr. Frank Yeigh.
Concert—The Salvation Army.
Chicken Dinner, given by Mrs. R. B. Hamilton, followed by Concert arranged by Messrs. Charles Ross and McCann.
Concert—Temple Baptist S.S.
Concert—Toc H. (two evenings).
Moving Pictures, etc.—St. Dunstan's Church.
Concert—Mr. W. J. Shaw and friends.
Concert—Bell Telephone Co., Parkdale Exchange.
Concert—Parkdale Presbyterian Choir.
Concert arranged by Mr. H. Wilson.
Concert—Brotherhood of St. Andrew.
Concert—Miss Mason and friends.
Concert arranged by Mr. C. A. Ward.
Concert—Canadian General Electric Co.
Entertainment by the Midway entertainers from National Exhibition.
Motor Ride, Tobacco and Candy—Ontario Motor League.
Canadian National Exhibition, free admission for patients and attendants.

SPECIAL DONATIONS

Inglis, Mrs. William—Wicker Furniture for Sitting-room.
Dale Estate—Flowers for Annual Meeting and Graduation.
Gundy, Mr. S. B.—100 copies Anglican Hymnals.
Emmett, Mr. Harry—Cleaning G. D. R. Walls—cost of $33.00.
Riordan, Mrs. Bruce L.—Framed portrait of late Dr. Bruce L. Riordan.
Needlework Guild of Canada—Large number articles of underwear.
Eaton Co. Limited—Box Fruit and Candy for each patient.
City Dairy Co. Limited—Ice Cream for household on several occasions.
Altschul, A. H. (New York)—Large outside doormat.
Chambers, C., Parks Commissioners—Flowers and Potted Plants.
Neilson, Mr. Allen—Ice Cream for household.
Salvation Army—Treat of Cake, etc.
Currie, E. & S. Co. Limited—Neckties. etc.
Miles, Mr. A. W.—Use of ambulance, also free burial for three patients.
Acheson, Mr.—Magazines.
Anglo-American Direct Tea Co.—5 lbs. Tea.
Brown, Mrs.—Rubber Tree.
Beatty, Mrs. W. H.—Pair Chickens.
Blake, Mrs. Hume—Pair Chickens.
Dods, Mrs.—Flowers.
Church of Epiphany—Flowers, Plants.
College Street United Church—Fruit, Flowers.
Cunningham, Mrs.—Magazines.
Dominion Fruit Board—Fruit, Vegetables.
Eberhard, Mrs.—Handkerchiefs.
Everist-Kirkpatrick, Limited—Case Holly, 3 Christmas Trees.
Hartz, J. F. Co.—Medical Supplies.
Ingram & Bell Limited—Drugs.
Kent, Mr. W. G.—250 Bulbs.
Kent, Mrs. Ambrose—2 cases Oranges.
Massey, Mrs. W. E. H.—2 large pictures.
Mara, Mr.—Wheel and Carrying Chair.
Nicholson, Mrs.—Wheel Chair.
National Club—Dishes.
Sparks, Mrs. Wm.—Grapes and 12 baskets Peaches.
Stanley Lodge—Flowers.
Standard Fuel Co. Limited—2 Turkeys.
Sloan, John & Co.—5 lbs. Chocolates
Smith, Misses—Case each Lemons and Oranges.
Tyrrell & Co.—Books.

SUBSCRIPTION LIST

Leonard, Lt.-Col. R.W.	$500.00
Neilson, Wm. Ltd.	265.00
City Dairy Co. Ltd.	200.00
Member of Board of Management	200.00
Lennox, E. J.	200.00
Relatives of the late Miss Ferry	169.50
Purdy, Mansell, Ltd.	150.00
Brown, R. L.	100.00
Flavelle, Sir Joseph	100.00
Firstbrook Bros. Ltd.	100.00
Holden, John B.	100.00
Kennedy, Thos.	100.00
Kent, Mrs. Ambrose	100.00
Larkin, P. C.	100.00
Michie, Col. J. F.	100.00
McKinnon, W.L. & Co.	100.00
Toronto Carpet Mfg. Co. Ltd.	100.00
Watt & Watt	100.00
Zetz Lodge, G.R.C. Florence Dobson Cot)	100.00
MacKay, Rev. (C. Miller Estate)	56.30
Aikens, Mrs. W. H. B.	50.00
Bredin, M.	50.00
Clark, Miss Mortimer	50.00
Cawthra, W. H.	50.00
Christie, Brown & Co., Ltd.	50.00
Davis, Hon. E. J.	50.00
Ely, E. F.	50.00
Emmett, Harry	50.00
Goodyear Tire & Rubber Co., Ltd.	50.00
Hutchison, Arch.	50.00
Kennedy, Thos.	50.00
Love, Mrs. H. H.	50.00
Macdonald, J. K.	50.00
McCarthy, Leighton	50.00
Rolph, Clark & Stone, Ltd.	50.00
Stone, William	50.00
Wood, Gundy & Co.	50.00
W. P. & F. B. M.	50.00
Wheatley, late Miss Edith	49.09
Northrop & Lyman Co. Ltd.	30.00
Aird, Sir John	25.00
Ames, A. E.	25.00
Adams Furniture Co., Ltd.	25.00
Ade, Edward	25.00
Blake, Mrs. Hume	25.00
Baird, W. A.	25.00
Bradshaw, A. & Son, Ltd.	25.00
Balm, H.	25.00
Brown Bros. Ltd.	25.00
Belle Ewart Ice Co.	25.00
Clarke, A. R. & Co.	25.00
Campbell, Miss Frances	25.00
Freyseng, Ed.	25.00
Georgina Lodge	25.00
Gundy, J. H.	25.00
Green, John C. & Co.	25.00
Howland, H. S. Sons & Co., Ltd.	25.00
Harding, C. V.	25.00
Ionic Lodge, G.R.C.	25.00
Kent, W. G.	25.00
Kent, McClain, Ltd.	25.00
Laidlaw, R. Lumber Co., Ltd.	25.00
Michie, Miss Effie	25.00
Mt. Sinai Lodge, A.F. & A.M.	25.00
McMurrich, G. Temple	25.00
Nairn, Miss Agnes	25.00
Oxford University Press	25.00
Parry, C. H.	25.00
Reed, Shaw & McNaught	25.00
Russell Motor Car Co.	25.00
Ryrie-Birks, Ltd.	25.00
Rathbone, Geo. Ltd.	25.00
Ruddy, Mrs. E. L.	25.00
Steele, W. D.	25.00
Steele Briggs Seed Co., Ltd.	25.00
Southam Press, Ltd.	25.00
Sproatt & Rolph	25.00
Tidy S. & Son, Ltd.	25.00
Victoria Harbour Lumber Co.	25.00
Warren, Mrs. H. D.	25.00
Woolworth, F. W. Co., Ltd.	25.00
Ashlar Lodge	20.00
Abbs, C. E.	20.00
Bristol, J. R. K.	20.00
Brodrick, P. W. D.	20.00
Dickie Construction Co Ltd.	20.00
Guest, Geo. E.	20.00
Hearst, Lady	20.00
Hobson, Mrs. E. J.	20.00
Laird, Mrs. Alex.	20.00
Link Belt, Ltd.	20.00
Moerschfelder, Mrs. Jas	20.00
Macdonald, Miss Bessie	20.00
Peterborough Masonic Board of Relief	20.00
Stauntons, Ltd.	20.00
Austin, A. W.	15.00
Bailey, A. H.	15.00
Barr, Walter H.	15.00
Canadian Bag Co.	15.00
Campbell, Graham	15.00
Gooderham, Mrs. A. E.	15.00
Heintzman, Gerhard, Ltd.	15.00
Jackes, Mrs.	15.00
Langton, W. A.	15.00
Nisbet & Auld	15.00
Pilkington Bros. Ltd.	15.00
Silks Ltd.	15.00
York Lodge, A.F. & A.M.	15.00
Armstrong, John J.	10.00
Aikenhead Hardware, Ltd.	10.00
Anderson, Dr. H. B.	10.00
Allison-Knox, Ltd.	10.00
Baker Advertising Co.	10.00
Burns, H. D.	10.00
Boulton, G. D.	10.00
Beverley, A.	10.00
Bennett & Elliott, Ltd.	10.00
Barker, H. C.	10.00
Brentnall, F. F.	10.00
Burgess, C. H. & Co.	10.00
Boeckh Co., Ltd.	10.00
Barber, Ellis, Ltd.	10.00
Can. Chewing Gum Co. Ltd.	10.00
Campbell, A. H.	10.00
Conger Lehigh Coal Co. Ltd.	10.00
Canada Printing Ink Co., Ltd.	10.00
Clark, P. M. & Son	10.00
Cowan Co., Ltd.	10.00
Cohen, J.	10.00
Carhartt, Hamilton, Cotton Mills, Ltd.	10.00
Cassells, Brock & Kelly	10.00
Credit Lodge, A.F. & A.M.	10.00
Deacon, Lt.-Col. F. H.	10.00
Ellis Bros. Ltd.	10.00
Goldman, L.	10.00
Grand River Lodge	10.00
Gillespie Fur Co., Ltd.	10.00
Gage, Wm. & Co., Ltd.	10.00
Gearing, Edward	10.00
Gray, Frank M.	10.00
Henderson, Mrs. Jos.	10.00
Hughes, D. E.	10.00
Imperial Extract Co.	10.00
Ivey, John D. & Co., Ltd.	10.00
Isabella, M.	10.00
Jones & Proctor Bros. Ltd.	10.00
J. T. H.	10.00
Kirkpatrick, A. M. M.	10.00
Lowe Brothers, Ltd.	10.00
Lee, Mr. and Mrs. Geo. M.	10.00
Muirhead, Geo. H.	10.00
Macklem, Mr. and Mrs. O.	10.00
Macdonald, Mrs. W. C.	10.00
Mack, C. W.	10.00
MacInnes, Mrs. B. S.	10.00
McQuillan, Thos.	10.00
McCarthy, Mrs. J.L.G.	10.00
Northway, John & Son, Ltd.	10.00
Orillia Lodge, A.F. & A.M.	10.00
Perry, Geo. D.	10.00
Rooke, H.	10.00
Rogers, Col. J. B.	10.00
Smith, Mrs. Harry T.	10.00
Stewart, W. Dunlop	10.00
Segsworth, R. F.	10.00
Taylor, J. & J., Ltd.	10.00
Touche, Geo. A. & Co.	10.00
Wilson, Col. R. S.	10.00
Wallace, Robert	10.00
American Hat Mfg. Co.	5.00
Acacia Lodge (Hamilton)	5.00
Alexander, W. J.	5.00
Amos, Rev. Walter	5.00
Bedford, E.	5.00
Barber, George	5.00
Brittain, Horace L.	5.00
Birrell, N. L.	5.00
Burrows, Acton, Ltd.	5.00
Bickersteth, J. B.	5.00
Berryman, Emerson & C	5.00
Chown, Rev. E.A. (late)	5.00
Coatsworth, Judge	5.00
Carrick, Mr. and Mrs. W. H.	5.00
Cons. Plate Glass Co. Ltd.	5.00

SUBSCRIPTION LIST—Continued

Dominion Paper Box Co..............	5.00	
Fleming, J. H....	5.00	
Friend, A......	5.00	
Gash, N. B.......	5.00	
Goldsmiths' Stock Co., Ltd.............	5.00	
Harwood, H. S........	5.00	
Hodgetts, Mrs. Harry.	5.00	
Hambly & Wilson, Ltd.	5.00	
Highgate Lodge, A.F. & A.M...........	5.00	
Lyman Bros. & Co. Ltd.	5.00	
Linc Brokerage Co. Ltd	5.00	
Milburn, T. H. Co. Ltd.	5.00	
Leclanc & Son......	5.00	
Munro, A. H........	5.00	
Nason, T. H........	5.00	
Nicholson, Geo. A.....	5.00	
Nerlich & Co.........	5.00	
Ontario Wind Engine & Pump Co..........	5.00	
Robertson, The Jas. Co. Ltd............	5.00	
Ryrie, Mrs. Harry....	5.00	
Saxby, R. M........	5.00	
Schnaufer, A. F. Co., Ltd.............	5.00	
Theatrical Mutual Association..........	5.00	
Van Norman, C. C....	5.00	
Burns, Edward Co., Ltd.............	3.00	
Dunlop Tire & Rubber Co., Ltd...	3.00	
Glenbinnie, S. S. (Kingston)............	3.00	
Tindall, W. B.....	3.00	
Lansdowne Lodge, S.O.C.............	2.50	
Clemes Bros..........	2.00	
Campbell, Miss Mary..	2.00	
Creighton, Miss Edith.	2.00	
Galena Signal Oil Co...	2.00	
Globe Printing Co.....	2.00	
Ingles, Ven. Archdeacon	2.00	
Jefferis, I.............	2.00	
McGinnis, Miss Mary (Craighurst)........	2.00	
Goodall, Miss Jessie...	1.00	
Joe The Marine.......	1.00	

$6,257.39